The Road Trip

Presented to:

_____

Love:

_____

Date:

_____

And you are complete in Him,
who is the head of all principality and power.

Colossians 2:10

First Edition, 2019

ISBN 978-1-7336927-0-0

Editing by Sean Fraser
Book design by Sean Fraser
Marketing strategy by Chelsea Fraser

TheRoadTripBook@gmail.com

Dedicated to He who gives grace.

Heartfelt gratitude to all my family who have blessed me with encouragement, love, and great joy! Thank you to everyone who has supported me in prayer through this journey, and to you, reader, as we travel the road together.

THE ROAD TRIP

A STORY + JOURNAL

CHERYL FRASER

road map

the empty road

The path we travel is our own individual journey. There is not a map or person that will guide our life expedition. Within each one of us God has placed himself to go before, guide, and never leave us. His assurance for this road trip called life is that, even if we have never walked into a church or read the Bible, He resides within us. It's a journey of trust, surrender, and belonging.

I understand the innate yearning to belong. Activities, adventures, and other people never satisfied that inner need. It could only be fulfilled by the one who placed the desire within. God gave everyone that yearning to seek and draw closer to Him. When I first was introduced to Jesus I didn't truly understand who He was and what He had done for us. It was only by learning about His character and love that I was able to trust Him in the driver's seat.

The Lord speaks on a personal level: *You are a chosen child, no one can take you away from me. Please know I look at you with love and adoration and want the best for you. Lean not on your own understanding; trust and depend on me. Wait, and let me reveal my love for you.*

So in Christ Jesus you are all
children of God through faith...

Galatians 3:26 NIV

braking

It all escalated when I was driving home from work the other night and a driver crossed over the line and hit me head on. Within seconds I had lost all control, a terrifying, yet impactful moment in my life. Through God's shield of protection I survived that accident without a physical scratch.

Although I got behind the wheel again, my confidence in myself had been broken. My confused heart knew there was something missing. The turmoil and questions had been building up. *How do I drive the course that had been set before me? What is my purpose? When I am at the end of myself, where do I go from there?*

I was becoming weak. And yet, that weakness was the beginning of a new dependence, strength, and relationship that would sustain me for the rest of my life.

Let us therefore come boldly
to the throne of grace,
that we may obtain mercy
and find grace to help in time of need.

Hebrews 4:16

embarking

When I began preparations for my road trip I felt excited about venturing into unknown territory. The packing seemed like an endless process. Piled-high were the possessions I presumed would be required for my journey. Being a novice traveler I thought that planning for every possible situation would protect me from any discomfort or inconvenience encountered. Clothes to cover myself, maps to show me the way, even candles for when I felt darkness. Little did I know my preparations could never change the plan already set out for me, and there was a far greater source of protection, direction, and light.

I stepped back, surveyed the pile, and pondered: is something missing? Forging ahead I continued to pursue my plan, assuming this would lead me down the right path. I embarked, confident in my course . . . how lost I already was.

For the Lord will be your confidence,
And will keep your foot from being caught.

Proverbs 3:26

I love those who love me,
And those who seek me diligently will find me.

Proverbs 8:17

baggage

The trunk was packed with so much baggage the seams were about to burst. After much reorganizing and rearranging I could just about slam the trunk closed! However, when I tried to pick up that last bag it was too heavy to even lift. I looked around for someone to help carry my burdens. Past life experiences and unrealistic expectations were crammed inside, building-up to inner chaos. Struggling and being dragged down by my own baggage was completely exhausting! Finally, recognizing I could not carry it alone, I called out for help. "Lord release me from this heavy burden" I cried, not knowing what that looked like, or what I truly even needed.

He said He gladly would, and graciously urged me to lighten my load. But the personal struggle and resistance of trying to let go was an intense battle. I hesitantly relinquished my burden, bit by bit, until I finally felt it lift. It was just a start, but now I knew I no longer needed to carry the weight alone.

Come to Me, all you who labor and are heavy laden,
and I will give you rest.
Take My yoke upon you and learn from Me,
for I am gentle and lowly in heart,
and you will find rest for your souls.
For My yoke is easy and My burden is light.

Matthew 11:28-30

rest stops

Due to heavy traffic, the first leg of my road trip took much
longer than expected. I was determined to reach my goal
and wanted to press on through the night, even if it totally
exhausted me. I certainly didn't see the value in stopping,
rest just seemed like another thing that would slow me down.
Then the white lines on the road started to become repetitive,
and anxiety started to creep into my mind. It wasn't until I
felt the violent bumps signaling I was crossing a lane that
I admitted to myself I needed to rest. So I found that it was
essential to exit the highway and yield to that unwanted rest
stop.

To be balanced and in alignment, food, rest, and refueling are required on any journey. I had lived my life in a constant race: always moving, continually wearing me down, not stopping to refuel. After struggling with the concept, I eventually recognized if I gave myself permission to rest God would renew my strength and enrich my life with a higher awareness of His voice. God continually reminds us to "rest in me," and understanding rest is not passive placed me in a position to yield to Him and receive His gifts.

Be still, and know that I am God...

Psalm 46:10

Lead me in Your truth and teach me,
For You are the God of my salvation;
On You I wait all the day.

Psalm 25:5

passengers

Oh, how passengers can be difficult on a long road trip. Simply assembling your group for travel can be an enormous task! I have come to recognize we are not on the same schedule; grace, love, and compassion are required as we travel down the road together. Everyone has their own specific needs and desires that must be addressed: window seat, temperature, music, etc. And just when your attention needs to be on the road come the many demands and opinions: bathroom, food, and urging you to go their direction. At times it makes you want to stop and jump out of the car! Focusing on His way, not allowing others to distract your course, will get you to your destination.

He will help you recognize that the passengers are the most treasured part of this journey. God has gifted you these passengers for a purpose, to value and travel down the road together. As for the backseat drivers, you know when you have one (or are one)! Their foot stamps down on the mat before you hit the brake. The next thing you hear is "you can go now the light is green" or "don't forget your signal." How utterly exhausting for both of you. These backseat drivers mostly evoke pain; creating tension in the car and tearing-down the drivers confidence. I guess I can relate to that backseat driver only too well. *If I were not giving directions where would we end up? Or maybe the driver would take a few wrong turns and get us lost?* Thinking we are in control gives a false sense of security in ourself, and I've gradually learned to not always have my hands on the wheel. There is only one who directs.

My dear brothers and sisters,
take note of this:
Everyone should be quick to listen,
slow to speak and slow to become angry,
because human anger does not produce
the righteousness that God desires.

James 1:19-20 NIV

speed

Speed limit and stop signs are posted for a reason. Nonetheless, I found myself accelerating, not wanting to let up on the gas, hurrying towards my perceived destination. Although I knew this could lead to consequences, penalty, and ultimately disaster, I continued pushing and pleasing, forging ahead in the fast lane without care for God's timing. The more I tried to get "there" in my own strength, the weaker and slower I became. After a while I began to understand there is no finish line. This allowed me to ease-up on the accelerator and travel at God's speed with Him by my side.

Trust in the Lord with all your heart,
And lean not on your own understanding;
In all your ways acknowledge Him,
And He shall direct your paths.

Proverbs 3:5-6

stuck in traffic

I was at a standstill. The particular road I chose was backed-up; everyone had somewhere to be but no one was progressing. The journey I was yearning for was one of growth, abundance, and forward momentum. This wasn't it! I needed to stop and reassess my route. *I thought this was the way Lord, I can see now its not the right way.* So I crept up to the closest exit and took the off ramp down an unfamiliar path. Doubts started to nag at me. *I feel so lost and alone. I'm taking the less traveled road and journeying on my own. I'm not sure of the way . . . Jesus, will you please help me?*

... the Lord your God, who went in the way before you to search out a place for you to pitch your tents, to show you the way you should go, in the fire by night and in the cloud by day.

Deuteronomy 1:32-33

Brethren, I do not count myself to have apprehended; but one thing I do, forgetting those things which are behind and reaching forward to those things which are ahead...

Philippians 3:13

Fuel

It had been hours since I took that unexpected exit and deviated from my original route, and the road before me was becoming more and more desolate. Panic and anxiety about whether this path was really getting me anywhere, and if this trip was what I should be doing with my time, continued to grow. I was beginning to consider turning around and going back to a comfortable road when the fuel light menacingly flicked on.

In the angry glow of that warning I stopped to consider my situation: I was miles from nowhere, far beyond the reach of cell service, with neither direction nor provision to move forward or even get me back to safety. I had no choice but to trust, and slowly began to creep along the road. With the last bit of fuel in the tank I rolled into a remote gas station.

I chatted with Jim, the cashier, and expressed my doubts about where this road would end up. Kindly, the older gentleman told me he had been down that road before and understood. He said that it could be a tricky road to maneuver and you could easily miss the turn: "some folks won't even attempt that road!" He encouraged me, even if it became challenging, to stay on the road to see where it leads me. Jim said it's ok to have doubts, questions, and ask for direction. I began to recognize this path I was traveling on was going to be a lifelong journey.

I pulled out of the station fueled-up, ready to press on and move forward.

Therefore comfort each other and edify one another,
just as you also are doing.

1 Thessalonians 5:11

pardon our dust

On long, open roads it's easy to get lost in thought. My mind began snagging on unforgiven actions, and times when I had been wronged or I wronged someone else. What then surfaced was a realization that I couldn't be set free from that pain on my own. But the road to forgiveness was not an easy one to travel, mainly because it required action on my part (and not someone else's). I had held on to the belief that I couldn't have redemption, and carried blame, pride, and resentment in my heart. This manifested itself in anxiety, anger, and illness. As I drove around that next curve in the road, I recognized it was time to relinquish that burden to God and ask for forgiveness and freedom that only He could supply! Through this process, I began to see that it wasn't all about me. Others were involved in the same struggle, even the people I had been hurt by. But when I forgave and released those burdens to Jesus I truly was set free!

I continued my journey filled with a new perspective on the road up ahead. We live in a fallen, imperfect world and there is a much bigger picture that we will not see on this side of eternity. That doesn't mean we can't have the abundant, joy-filled, complete life that Christ has given us today!

...bearing with one another,
and forgiving one another,
if anyone has a complaint against another;
even as Christ forgave you,
so you also must do.

Colossians 3:13

detour

But I wanted to take this road!

My GPS was programed for a specific schedule and destination. I had calculated just how long the drive would be. The route and sights I would see along the way were carefully mapped-out. Then the inevitable happened . . . road construction. I had to take a different route. The idea of a detour seemed torturous. Fear, frustration and stress seemed to envelop me as I approached this new route. How do I make such a drastic change in my road trip? I felt completely derailed. At first, I prayed that my path would be reopened but nothing changed. I was tempted to stop and pull-over, but then the voice inside instructed me to keep driving, He would give me direction. It was frustrating to let go of my plans, but eventually I turned the car down the new path and began to drive. *I don't know where the new road leads, Lord, but I trust you.* My grip began to loosen on the steering wheel and, not allowing circumstances to overcome my peace of mind, I was directed back to Jesus. I asked God for acceptance and strength to help navigate this new direction, and received guidance and wisdom to continue moving forward. Slowly the path started to unfold and I was led on a new journey. Although it felt long and lonely, Jesus promised He would guide me through the detour and never leave me. This route may not have been the original one I planned, but I trusted He always knew where it would end up.

"For I know the plans I have for you," declares the Lord, "plans to prosper you and not to harm you, plans to give you hope and a future."

Jeremiah 29:11 NIV

Now may the God of hope fill you with all joy and peace in believing, that you may abound in hope by the power of the Holy Spirit.

Romans 15:13

jammed gear

It seemed others were just cruising on by, yet I still couldn't

get it in gear. I was stuck in neutral. I struggled with the gear

shift but wasn't able to move. Finally I admitted to myself

that there was no quick fix and maintenance was needed.

I focused on Jesus, His character, and His promises. By

spending time in His presence I began to know him, and

realized He was molding me into His image. The relationship

that was being developed was one that influenced my

life more than any human relationship ever could. I

started to become the new creation He intended me to be.

Losing myself to Christ was frightening, I had held onto

independence and control for so many years, but I asked

myself, "what am I really losing?" Guilt, pain, worry, pride, confusion, the list goes on and on. Scary as it may seem, when I lost self I gained Him and all the treasures He had for me! Gradually, I started to build-up speed, passing by fear, anxiety, and lack of confidence. Now, I no longer needed to make comparisons or be envious as others sped by, because I had found my identity in Christ!

Therefore, if anyone is in Christ, he is a new creation;
old things have passed away;
behold, all things have become new.

2 Corinthians 5:17

road angel

As the sunset glistened a golden hue on the rolling hills of wheat I continued driving on the quiet, serene road. I was still quite a distance from my evening destination and darkness descended. What I could see on the road ahead started to become very dim, and then everything went black. That's when I realized my headlights had gone out. What was so peaceful and clear in the light became ominous traveling in darkness, all alone in the middle of nowhere. I drove slowly, as trying to make out the curves in the road was nearly impossible. I saw in my rear view mirror that a large semi truck was approaching from behind, and fear riveted through me as I wondered if the driver would see me!

He did, and must have understood my circumstances as he slowed behind me and, with powerful headlights shining over my diminutive car, guided me through the darkness. We drove around winding bends, up and down the rolling hills, something I never could have navigated on my own. As we approached the glow of a welcoming town I pulled over and waved in appreciation as the truck passed by and disappeared into the night. I looked up to the starry sky, recognizing guardian angels do exist and this one took the form of a truck driver.

Are they not all ministering spirits
sent forth to minister for those who will inherit salvation?

Hebrews 1:14

stopover

I pulled into a small, quaint town. The banner on main street announced it was Homecoming Week. I drove around and found myself drawn to a church, and when I walked in people welcomed me with open arms. They were setting up the banquet hall for the week's festivities and had some jobs for me to do . . . so wanting to belong I rolled up my sleeves and dug in. I worked continually that week side by side with these good people, but I was growing tired and with the tasks piling-up I began to wonder if I could ever do enough. It wasn't until one day I wandered into the chapel sat down and Jesus met me there.

He assured me of His love, belonging, and let me know I never had to prove my worthiness. This was a free gift He was offering me! I questioned Him: you mean I don't have to work for it, just receive it? His answer was yes.

I stayed in town for a while to serve Him, but I did so with a new awareness. I realized I was working for the Lord, and those jobs He equipped me for became joys! When it was time to hit the road again my new friends sent me off with prayer and blessings, knowing I had a journey to continue. They reminded me the church door was always open wherever I traveled, and the head of the church, Jesus, would always be in.

And whatever you do, do it heartily,
as to the Lord and not to men,
knowing that from the Lord you will receive
the reward of the inheritance;
for you serve the Lord Christ.

Colossians 3:23-24

snow

My journey continued and the road began to wind up a steep mountain pass. As I began the ascent I cherished the excitement of seeing the first snow flurries hit my windshield. My tires paved the first trail in the newly-fallen snow. I stopped and jumped out of the car to make a mandatory snow angel, laying there for a moment in the silence of a still world blanketed in white.

Carefully, I chained-up for the icy conditions and continued the climb, unaware that my preparations for the inclement weather wouldn't protect me from the trials ahead.

From the chamber of the south comes the whirlwind,
And cold from the scattering winds of the north.

Job 37:9

Have I not commanded you? Be strong and of good
courage; do not be afraid, nor be dismayed, for the Lord
your God is with you wherever you go.

Joshua 1:9

accident

Life's storms make the road challenging to navigate. We pray to stay safe and not encounter any accidents, although some are unavoidable. Hitting black ice can be scary, it can even cause you to swerve, lose control, and go off the road. Shock and grief can immobilize us. During this season life may seem to crash down around us. Whatever the circumstances are, help is always present on this road trip called life. At times it can be so difficult to make that 911 call; fear, pride and judgement can block us from wanting to seek assistance. Time and time again I've tried to handle these situations on my own, but eventually I learned that the only way through the chaos is to call out for help.

Sometimes it's just to fill up my tank and get back on the road. Other situations require a lot more assistance. Anxiety, lack of confidence, and fear can be all-consuming. It can be hard getting back in the car again . . . let alone drive!

I surveyed the car, there had been some damage, but in time those dents and scratches would be healed. The Lord assured me He had gone before me to give direction and guidance. Even on the darkest roads traveled I was not alone. My dependence on Jesus was developing, and I learned it was okay to ask for help. He was driving me through unknown territory, and all that was required of me was to wait on Him. Through faith and trust in Him, Jesus pulled me out of the icy ditch.

But from there you will seek the Lord your God,
and you will find Him if you seek Him
with all your heart and with all your soul.

Deuteronomy 4:29

For God has not given us a spirit of fear,
but of power and of love and of a sound mind.

2 Timothy 1:7

seatbelt

I got back into the car and fastened the seatbelt around my
body. I rely on the protection of the seatbelt, just like I yearn
for my heart and mind to be secure and safe. No device
or person can provide that kind of security. Just like the
seatbelt's physical provision I want His truth to be second
nature to provide mindful security. He says He will never
leave us or forsake us. That is a provision and promise I feel
secure in. So, on the mountainous roads or in the valley,
Jesus is with us making our fears on the road diminish.

And the Lord, He is the One who goes before you. He will be with you, He will not leave you nor forsake you; do not fear nor be dismayed.

Deuteronomy 31:8

do not enter

I never intended to exit the road I was on, but this one caught my eye. I was tempted by my desire to see where it would take me, so I turned. I justified my decision thinking I wanted a more scenic route. I was now heading in a direction I thought I would never go. The sign said rough road ahead! It seemed alright as I started out, but then I began to hit potholes.

I cried out for help, recognizing I couldn't do it on my own, asking the Holy Spirit to intercede for me. My state of weakness forced me to be dependent on the Lord. The concept of surrendering to Him and denying myself was foreign and challenging. It took waiting in His presence to receive His power to move forward. The Holy Spirit guided me to the truth; I was made aware of my sin and desperate need for help, then Jesus gave me the power to turn away from sin. As I surrendered, repented, and relinquished my will, I began to feel peace. It was still a struggle, but He promised me I would be able to withstand it. I am becoming familiar with this process. There have been, and will be, wrong turns in my life. Thankfully I have Jesus and His Grace!

For sin shall not have dominion over you,
for you are not under law but under grace.

Romans 6:14

No temptation has overtaken you except such as is
common to man; but God is faithful, who will not allow
you to be tempted beyond what you are able,
but with the temptation will also make the way of escape,
that you may be able to bear it.

1 Corinthians 10:13

Foothills

When I reached the mountain summit I was greeted with a majestic view. The road I was on wound through the foothills before me and gradually grew fainter until it vanished somewhere on the horizon. I pulled-over and grabbed my camera to try and capture the landscape. The image I saw through my viewfinder hardly did the scene justice, and I realized what I could see would always be but a fraction of the bigger picture God sees. I long to see that clear, grand scheme, but I've learned to trust Him even as the road before me disappears into the unknown. I began my descent, and slowly the snow gave way to meadows and tulips pushing their way up through the frosty fields. I opened my window and breathed in the fresh air, feeling renewal within.

Behold, I will do a new thing,
Now it shall spring forth;
Shall you not know it?
I will even make a road in the wilderness
And rivers in the desert.

Isaiah 43:19

missing the turn

I had been down this road so many times before so I knew I would not miss the turn this time. Feeling confident, I forged ahead and left the map folded in the glovebox. And yet here I was, circling around in confusion, realizing I had missed the turn and was repeating the same mistakes and feeling unsettled. I found myself in an environment that I could not handle on my own, needing to learn something I thought I already knew. So once again, I humbled myself to the Lord for the same thing I had so many times before, calling out for help to stop this pattern in my life. Eventually, I paused long enough to listen for guidance and heard a gentle voice stating "follow me."

As I circled back around the road I was able to reposition my thoughts on Jesus, the truth, and gain a healthy perspective on life situations. It seems just when we think we've got it, God reveals a lesson that must be relearned and revisited, and he gently reviews His truth with us. Being dependent on The Lord is never a sign of weakness or lack of knowledge, instead it's an opportunity to continually be in relationship with Him. My obedience to listen for His voice is slowly developing, and the time it takes to turnaround back to Jesus is lessening.

Therefore humble yourselves under the mighty hand of God, that He may exalt you in due time.

1 Peter 5:6

For God is not the author of confusion but of peace, as in all the churches of the saints.

1 Corinthians 14:33

desert

This new road I was traveling on was a long, slow road where there really wasn't much to see. It was actually quite boring, with miles of dry, depleted land where everything looked the same. Definitely not like the roads I would normally choose to take. I obediently kept driving in the direction Jesus was leading me. As I continued, the beauty of this drive started to unfold before me. I began to see things in a different light. The sun glistened on the sagebrush, allowing each individual branch to be seen. Its intricacy was beautiful. This reminded me of the people God placed in my life. Each one was unique, beautiful, and served a special purpose.

Something was starting to change within. What I once viewed as dull and monotonous now began to bring a steadfast, peaceful, feeling I had never experienced before. I wasn't familiar with a path like this, but I began to appreciate the slow pace, growth, and reflective time on the road.

Therefore, my beloved brethren, be steadfast, immovable,
always abounding in the work of the Lord,
knowing that your labor is not in vain in the Lord.

1 Corinthians 15:58

vacancy

Vacancy beckoned the illuminated sign, the light encouraging me to stop. The motel was simple, clean and welcoming; an unassuming row of red doors with large, bold numbers on them. It seemed like a place that had offered refuge for thousands of weary travelers over the years. Despite a nice hot shower and comfortable bed I laid awake with sleep evading me. Eager for something to tire my mind, I leaned over, opened the drawer and found the bible. I hadn't spent much time actually reading the bible. In my life it had always been something to dust on the nightstand or dutifully open when instructed in various churches. But as I read in that sparse, freeway-side room, the bible drew me in and the words came alive. It was uncanny how the scripture pertained to me personally, the passages seemingly addressing unique circumstances in my life (actually it felt a little alarming). The Holy Spirit was speaking to me. I read for hours that night, experiencing the word of God, before falling asleep.

The next morning as I gathered my belongings I knew that something had changed, the words I had read that previous night had pierced my heart and soul. Eager to keep reading, I stopped by the front desk and asked if I might purchase that bible for the rest of my journey. She told me that it was not available for purchase, it was a free gift.

For the word of God is living and powerful,
and sharper than any two-edged sword,
piercing even to the division of soul and spirit,
and of joints and marrow,
and is a discerner of the thoughts and intents of the heart.

Hebrews 4:12

turning

As I drove in silence along the highway I began to digest what I had read and what Christ had done for us. He died in my place to take away my sin and the sins of the world. His blood shed on the cross saved me! What a revelation to think about. God wants none to perish but all to receive the free gift of eternal life. As many times as I've heard this truth, it had never really sunk in. Now, I was hearing it loud and clear: the pain, torture, ridicule and personal sacrifice Jesus had suffered was for all mankind! I was being invited into an everlasting relationship that would endure through eternity. As I cruised on the open road that afternoon I said Yes, I believed in Christ and all He had done for us. I had just turned the corner on the road called belief!

For God so loved the world
that He gave His only begotten Son,
that whoever believes in Him should not perish
but have everlasting life.

John 3:16

The Lord is not slack concerning His promise,
as some count slackness, but is longsuffering toward us, not
willing that any should perish but that all should come to
repentance.

2 Peter 3:9

slowdown

I wish I could say the transformation in Christ was immediate and evident in all areas of my life. For me it was not that way, it was a slow process of surrender and dependence with a new awareness of Christ's presence. There was a certainty of how I wanted to live my life: with Jesus, in His truth, putting my hope and trust in Him. I yearned for some transformation in my life, yet I knew I was powerless without the Holy Spirit's help. After years of living independently, the willingness to allow the Holy Spirit to intercede on my part was welcomed. I no longer had to drive that road alone. I now had the assurance in Christ, and the unfailing relationship we had together!

And do not be conformed to this world,
but be transformed by the renewing of your mind,
that you may prove what is that good and acceptable
and perfect will of God.

Romans 12:2

driver's license

I pulled into a quaint roadside market, it was time to replenish my road food supply. When asked for my ID to confirm I was the credit card holder I realized it was missing from its usual spot. I turned every pocket and bag inside out but to no avail, a moment of panic set in. I had always placed so much value in my identity, and now it felt lost. It would have to be replaced.

The question was, what would it be replaced with? Normally I would have jumped into a new activity or job to fill that void, but I had grown in the knowledge of no longer needing those titles and labels to define who I was.

It had been quite a journey but the old self had been dying and I was a new creation in Christ. I was now sealed with a new identity that was liberating and freeing from the bonds of my past. It felt like I was having a second chance on life and was being born again.

After retracing my steps back to the parking lot, I found my drivers license laying next to the car door. I was glad to have found that piece of ID, but throughout this journey, my perception of my identity had changed!

That which is born of the flesh is flesh,
and that which is born of the Spirit is spirit.

John 3:6

But whoever is united with the Lord
is one with him in spirit.

1 Corinthians 6:17 NIV

cruising

Traveling forward on my journey I felt an exuberance that I hadn't experienced in a long time. Once again, I was cruising the road with clarity and direction; I felt complete in Him.

Placing Jesus in the driver's seat brought peace and contentment to my soul. It was a time for joy, so I cranked-up my music and began to sing praise! I accelerated with ease and headed for a special vista. He guided me as I cruised around the corner of a rocky coastline, then a spectacular sight unfolded ahead of me. I pulled over and paused in awe of the vast ocean. I reflected, recognizing God's sovereignty and phenomenal creation. *If God created this, He could certainly guide me through my challenges. Lord, please help me to glorify and focus on you. When the road gets rough and I am confused help me to stop, rest, and ask for directions. If there is a blind spot, open my eyes and guide me with your clarity. When I turn away from you Jesus, direct me back to You and your way.*

Getting out of the car and walking towards the beach the sound of the waves methodically cleansed my soul. I stood in peace, feeling God's grace, love, and presence encompass me.

This is the day the Lord has made;
We will rejoice and be glad in it.

Psalm 118:24

I love the Lord, because He has heard
My voice and my supplications.
Because He has inclined His ear to me,
Therefore I will call upon Him as long as I live.

Psalm 116:1-2

are we there yet ?

It's human nature to want to achieve a goal. For so long I strived to understand the route God had set for me, asking "are we there yet?" when things remained unclear. But now I've learned there will always be uncharted roads ahead, and I've grown content in simply traveling with Jesus, thankful to be on a continued journey together.

Hopping back into the car, I glanced in the rearview mirror and saw my reflection. I recognized that every bend in the road held a specific purpose that had been personalized and created for me to travel through. It was a journey I could not have imagined, it was something greater!

Not that I have already attained,
or am already perfected; but I press on,
that I may lay hold of that for which Christ Jesus
has also laid hold of me.

Philippians 3:12

destination

God yearns for a relationship with us and He has the utmost compassion, grace, and mercy. The time spent developing an intimate relationship with Jesus prepares us for when we turn that corner for eternity with Him. It has been a long haul learning to treasure the journey, and now I know my destination and the way to my heavenly home. With great anticipation I look forward to getting there, but I don't want to miss the abundant joys of being present today on the road trip of life.

I've never been one for collecting souvenirs, but what I did gather on this individual journey was belonging, unconditional love, wisdom, and truth to carry throughout my life travels. The Greatest Guide had placed these treasured gifts before me, and I learned that my sense of belonging and completion only came through Him. I needed to go no further.

For by grace you have been saved through faith,
and that not of yourselves; it is the gift of God...

Ephesians 2:8

Jesus said to him, "I am the way, the truth, and the life.
No one comes to the Father except through Me."

John 14:6

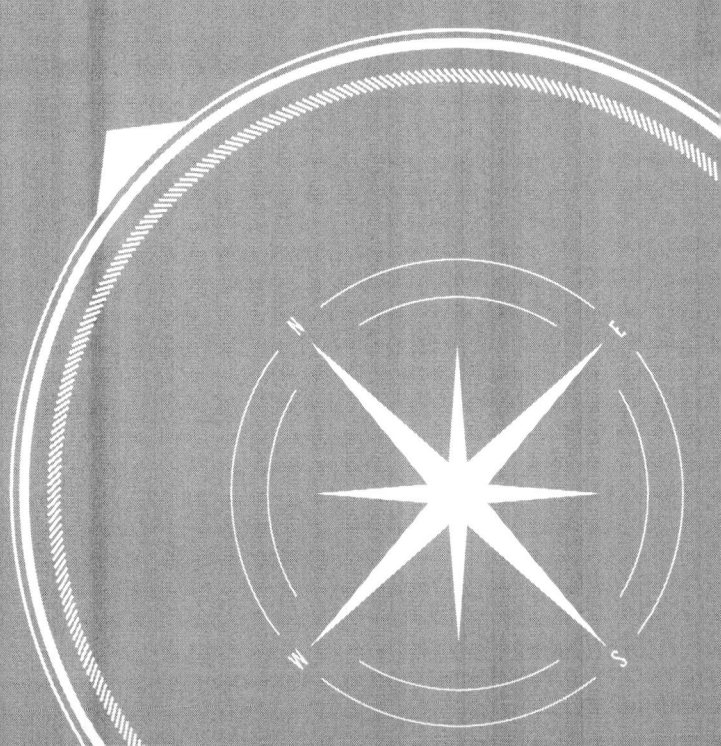

epilogue

The travel guidebook for all of life's journeys - filled with encouragement, guidance, and truth - is the Bible. My prayer is the Word will direct and empower you on the road trip of life.

CONVERSATION
STARTERS

1. What chapter resonated the most with you in this writing?

2. When you are at the end of yourself, where do you find strength?

3. Where have you felt you belonged? Did this feeling of belonging last?

4. Is there baggage weighing you down? How can you lighten your load?

5. Do you establish boundaries for rest? Is this advantageous?

6. Do you feel your identity comes from your work or some other area of performance in your life?

7. What does Jesus mean to you?

8. Do you feel some passengers are steering you away from God? How do you create boundaries in this area?

9. Have you ever found yourself forging ahead and not waiting on God's timing?

10. It's okay to ask for help! God places people in our lives for a reason. Are you comfortable with seeking assistance in a trusted person?

11. Does it ever seem to you that others are just cruising through life and you can't seem to get it in gear?

12. Has there been someone that had a positive influence in your life? How did that person direct you?

13. How have you responded when your plans didn't work out?

14. In what way has your dependence on the Lord grown?

15. What does it mean to surrender to the Lord? What do you have to relinquish?

16. How have we been set free from sin? How has this impacted your life?

17. How can we change destructive patterns in our life?

18. Discuss a season of joy in your life!

19. In what ways have the Bible verses in this writing spoken to you?

20. What does it mean to be complete In Christ?

The LORD bless you and keep you;
The LORD make His face shine upon you,
And be gracious to you;
The LORD lift up His countenance upon you,
And give you peace.

Numbers 6:24-26

Finally, brethren, whatever things are true, whatever things are noble, whatever things are just, whatever things are pure, whatever things are lovely, whatever things are of good report, if there is any virtue and if there is anything praiseworthy— meditate on these things. The things which you learned and received and heard and saw in me, these do, and the God of peace will be with you.

Philippians 4:8-9

So I said, "Oh, that I had wings like a dove! I would fly away and be at rest."

Psalm 55:6

But from there you will seek
the Lord your God,
and you will find Him if you seek Him
with all your heart and with all your soul.

Deuteronomy 4:29

Trust in Him all times, you people;
Pour out your heart before Him;
God is a refuge for us.

Psalm 62:8

All we like sheep have gone astray;
We have turned, every one, to his own way;
And the Lord has laid on Him
the iniquity of us all.

Isaiah 53:6

For the law of the Spirit of life
in Christ Jesus has made me free
from the law of sin in death.

Romans 8:2

These things I have spoken to you,
that in Me you have peace.
In the world you will have tribulation;
but be of good cheer,
I have overcome the world.

John 16:33

The Lord your God in your midst,
The Mighty One, will save;
He will rejoice over you with gladness,
He will quiet you with His love,
He will rejoice over you with singing.

Zephaniah 3:17

Stand fast therefore in the liberty
by which Christ has made us free,
and do not be entangled again
with a yoke of bondage.

Galatians 5:1

Now it came to pass in those days
that He went out to the mountain to pray,
and continued all night
in prayer to God.

Luke 6:12

In this manner, therefore, pray;

Our Father in heaven,

Hallowed be Your name.

Your kingdom come.

Your will be done

On earth as it is in heaven.

Give us this day our daily bread.

And forgive us our debts,

As we forgive our debtors.

And do not lead us into temptation,

But deliver us from the evil one.

For Yours is the kingdom and the power

and the glory forever.

Amen.

Matthew 6:9-15

But as many as received Him,
to them He gave the right
to become children of God,
to those who believe in His name:

John 1:12

But may the God of all grace,
who called us to His eternal glory
by Christ Jesus, after you have suffered a while,
perfect, establish, strengthen
and settle you. To Him be the glory
and the dominion forever and ever.
Amen.

1 Peter 5:10-11

Now may the God of hope
fill you with all joy and peace in believing,
that you may abound in hope
by the power of the Holy Spirit.

Romans 15:13

If any of you lacks wisdom,
let him ask of God,
who gives to all liberally
and without reproach,
and it will be given to him.

James 1:5

As many as I love,
I rebuke and chasten.
Therefore be zealous and repent.

Revelation 3:19

For you did not receive
the spirit of bondage again to fear,
but you received the Spirit of adoption
by whom we cry out, "Abba, Father."

Romans 8:15

Behold, I stand at the door and knock.
If anyone hears My voice and opens the door,
I will come into him and dine with him,
and he with Me.

Revelation 3:20

And He said to me, "My grace is sufficient for you, for My strength is made perfect in weakness."

2 Corinthians 12:9

Finally, brethren, farewell.
Become complete.
Be of good comfort, be of one mind,
live in peace;
and the God of love and peace
will be with you.

2 Corinthians 13:11

Made in the USA
Middletown, DE
27 November 2021